The 'ad' Dad

By Viola & Zaida Stefano

VeeZee Publications

Copyright © VeeZee Publications Pty. Ltd. 2024

First published in Australia in 2024
by VeeZee Publications Pty. Ltd.

veezeepublications.com

The right of Viola Stefano to be identified as the author of this work have been asserted by her in accordance with the **Copyright Amendment (Moral Rights) Act 2000.**

All rights reserved. Apart from any use as permitted by the author & under the **Copyright Act 1968**, no part may be reproduced, copied, scanned, stored in a retrieval system, recorded, or shared, by any means or in any form, without prior written & signed authorization from the publisher.

ISBN: 978-1-923120-12-9

A catalogue record of this book is available from the **National Library of Australia.**

Author: Viola Stefano
Illustrations, cover & internal designs: Zaida Stefano

Illustrations copyright © Zaida Stefano 2024
Design copyright © Zaida Stefano 2024

Disclaimer: The content presented in this book is meant for educational purposes only. The author & publisher claim no accountability to any entity or person for any liability, damage, or loss caused or assumed to be caused directly or indirectly as a consequence of the application, use, or interpretation of the material in this book.

Core words used in this book

I	**want**	**can**	stop	**look**
like	more	**he**	go	see
here	what	do	**the**	**and**
out	where	we	it	up
not	they	when	that	down
she	**now**	them	**is**	put
help	off	**you**	yes	**on**
turn	**who**	**this**	no	why
done	**make**	**a**	**to**	under
come	**in**	some	which	there
open	**get**	**good**	same	home

Brad is a water dragon who can be bad.

He's covered and clad

in green and brown.

Brad sits on a lily pad and looks at dad with a frown.

Dad looks at him and growls, "Bad, Brad!"

Brad turns and jumps into the dam.

He swims a lap, and dad gets mad.

"I want you to come here NOW, Brad!"

"I'm done with this! You make me sad."

"I'm really sorry dad!"

Brad is a water dragon who can be good.

Dad is a water dragon who can be glad.

Words with 'ad' in this book

dad	Brad	bad
glad	mad	pad
clad	sad	

Words with a short 'a' sound in this book

dragon	at	lap
dam	can	and

Learning made easy with VeeZee

VeeZee Publications

Wait, there's more!

Visit our website for information about our range of readers
& supporting products.

veezeepublications.com

www.ingramcontent.com/pod-product-compliance
Lightning Source LLC
Chambersburg PA
CBHW042107090526

44590CB00004B/120